SCALES OUT OF BALANCE

May your scales weigh heavy with good fortune.

Larry Schug

SCALES OUT OF BALANCE

Lawrence Schug

NORTH STAR PRESS OF ST. CLOUD, INC.

Dedicated
to the memory of my father and mother
and to Juli
my wife;
She speaks the language of orchids

Thanks for help along the way—
Barton Sutter, Sr. Kristin Malloy, J. F. Powers,
Tom Finnegan, Sr. Andre Marthaler, Mike Opitz
and Sr. Colman O'Connell

Cover photo: Steven A. Page
Back cover photo: Don Bruno

ISBN: 0-87839-062-6

Printed in the United States of America by Park Press, Inc., Waite Park, Minnesota.

Published by:
North Star Press of St. Cloud, Inc.
P.O. Box 451
St. Cloud, Minnesota 56302

CONTENTS

The following poems were originally published in the listed magazines:

"Barber's Son" and "Hobo Camp," *Rag Mag*, vol. 7, no. 1, 1989.
"Second Shift" and "Rose-breasted Grosbeaks," *American Knight*, vol. 1, no. 1, 1990.
"Baseball Fan," *Manna*, vol. 9, no. 1, 1988.
"The Bandshell," *Z Miscellaneous*, vol. 2, no. 4, 1988.
"Bread Bowl," *Z Miscellaneous*, vol. 1, no. 3, 1987.
"The Roots Know," *Z Miscellaneous*, vol. 1, no. 4, 1987.
"A Field of Black-eyed Susans," *Z Miscellaneous*, vol. 2, no. 2, 1988.
"Two-bit Ella," *Studio 1*, no. 13, 1989.
"Jumprope," "The Giants and the Dodgers," and "Cork," *Studio 1*, no. 14, 1990.
"Eggs," *Diotima*, vol. 11, no. 4, 1990.
"Blue Shoes," *Diotima*, vol. 11, no. 1, 1990.
"Eleven Days after the Abduction of Jacob Wetterling," *Diotima*, vol. 11, no. 2, 1990.
"Folks Forget," *Diotima*, vol. 10, no. 3, 1989.
"I Know Somebody," *Diotima*, vol. 9, no. 2, 1988.
"A Turtle Poem," *Diotima*, vol. 10, no. 2, 1989.
"Sunday on Friday Night," *Diotima*, vol. 11, no. 4, 1990.
"Jake in the Sun" and "A Testimony Against the Witch of St. Wendel," *Another Place to Publish*, vol. 3, no. 4, 1989.
"Dairy Farmers," *Loonfeather*, Spring 1988.
"Candlemaker's Suicide" and "Crops that Grow in a Drought," *Pegasus*, 1988.
"Foreclosure Auction," *A Hard Row to Hoe*, vol. 1, no. 4, 1989.
"In Johnson's Pasture," *Kana*, Winter 1989.
"school bell," *Plainsongs*, vol. 10, no. 1, 1989.
"The Animals at Margaret's Farm," *Writer's Journal*, July 1989.
"Geese," *Lower Stumpf Lake Review*, vol. 15, 1990.
"White Bread," *Lower Stumpf Lake Review*, vol. 15, 1990.

Unknown

Barber's Son

We used to talk at haircut time,
My pa and I,
Just like the men at the barbershop.
While the clipper buzzed around my head
He told me jokes and stories
About the old days,
His young days;
And I told him the crazy things that I had done.
He shook his head,
"Ya," he said,
"I was wild like that too, son."

The ball game on the radio;
We listened to talk of double plays and RBIs
And pop flies hit as high as the sky.
When the slugger struck out, we cussed him,
But next time up, he socked one,
And we forgave him.
Without words, we forgave each other too;
For absences and failures,
Weakness and embarrassment,
Errors and missed signals,
Messed-up plays and losing streaks.

Our silence said things, though,
Deep things
That men could never say aloud.
He spoke with gentle hands
Flitting around my head like birds,
And I answered
With a glance at his face in the mirror.

Second Shift

The waitress at home, tired, footsore,
Cries a little, then cooks supper
Seasoned with sighs and sobs,
But served with a smile,
Better than her best restaurant smile.
She makes us feel like big tippers,
Squeezes my shoulders,
Hugs my little brother's neck,
Calls us honey and brings us pie,
As if we are truckers
Waiting for a drunken storm,
Swerving toward us on the highway.

The Giants and the Dodgers

On a vacant lot by the railroad tracks,
No one watches the Giants and Dodgers
Play a quadruple-header (with a break for supper)
Except the passengers on the Prairie Flyer.
On a diamond with plywood bases and
A backstop built of bicycles,
Willie Mays and Duke Snider
Share a Hank Aaron glove and
A nailed-together Mickey Mantle bat;
An old nag of a baseball's floppy hide
Whirrs with every pitch.

The Giants and the Dodgers
Babysit each others' little brothers;
The big kids call 'em little shits,
Make 'em shag foul balls and wild pitches.
Between "at bats," the big boys give lessons
In swearin' and spittin' and gripping a ball,
And how to give the finger to the Flyer,
Full of old shortstops and catchers
Leaving this minor-league town like a line drive,
Forgotten as a foul ball
When the next batter pounds the plate.

Cork

No Irish funeral, this.
No house crowded with women wailing.
A Minnesota German mourns alone,
Speaks in silence to his dead brother
Of things old German men never say aloud.
But his brother's name is a cork
That will not sink;
It floats to the surface of speech again.
Maybe one more drink.

My Old Man's Devil

My old man held his devil down
For twenty dry years.
There were times, my old man said,
When the devil whispered words
From which he could not hide,
Words that almost made my old man
Loosen his grip on his devil's neck.

My old man told me there were many nights
The devil came 'round, spoilin' for a fight.
He said the devil fights dirty,
And the devil likes to kill you
One heartbeat at a time.
Pa's hand tightened around his coffee cup.
The devil never gives up, he said.

My old man flexed sinewy muscles,
Muscles that were weak when he was young,
But grew strong as oak limbs, after
His skin had wrinkled like bark.
My old man and his devil died,
They died on the same day,
But the devil died first; of thirst.

Sunday on Friday Night

My old man forced me to wishing.
When I was young, I wished for him
To always be like he was on Sunday mornings,
When he held me as tight as he held that bottle
That made me invisible to him on Friday night.
Now, I know he couldn't be Sunday on Friday night,
Though he craved his son
Like blood craves muscle and bone.

Now that my father is dead,
I know he did embrace me, a shadow embrace.
I know, because I live downstream
In the same desert river bed where he lived;
Where men have learned to live dry lives.
But dams do break, and rivers do rage
Through sun-baked gullies eroded in topskin,
When flood is least expected.

Baseball Fan

A cold chrome bed
In an antiseptic November hospital,
Surrounded by strangers dressed in white
Is not a good place to die.
The mocking lights of telemetric monitors,
Digits and graphs,
Flash and blink on your skin,
Red and green and blue.
No, you should have died at home,
On a Sunday afternoon
Early in May,
When the baseball season was new.
You should have been sitting at the kitchen table,
Coffee cup and pipe at hand,
Basking in the broadcast
Of a double-header.

The flies are buzzing on the back door screen.
The announcer drones.
The crowd murmurs like Baseball Buddhists chanting "Om."
The pitcher lets loose with a wicked curve.
The batter swings and
Lofts a high fly ball
To deepest centerfield.
Your soul joins the sphere
On its skyward climb;
As the ball falls back to earth,
Your chin drops to your chest, your body sags.
The Centerfielder gathers in your soul
Using two hands.
The final out,
The inning is over.

Hobo Camp

After supper, late in the fall,
When cold stars filled the sky,
I snuck over to the hobo camp
To spy.

I listened to men cuss and shout
Like laughing, drunken crows
At a feast of highway stew,
And once in a while, punches flew.
I heard words about California
From the mouths of ravens
Who live by the railroad tracks;
They talked of brown Juanita
Lying on her back.
They talked in miles and places,
Never spoke a word of time,
My eyes turned to follow a shooting star
While listening to Shorty's rhyme;
About the moon left behind on the rails
On the prairie west of Fargo,
The sun going underground
In the shadows above Chicago;
How riding the rails is rough, and it's cold,
And how he'll keep riding these boxcars and
Prob'ly die in their hold.

I snuck away and ran for home,
Like autumn leaves rattling down the street,
To a night of rocky, rumbling sleep.
I dreamed my feet hung from a boxcar door.
I had the morning and the mountains
And a bottle of May apple wine.

The Bandshell

They say the bandshell
Isn't safe enough for Sousa anymore,
The orchestra must play from folding chairs,
Tilted, legs stuck in the ground.
Written on the walls inside,
The graffiti of town boys,
The names of town girls,
Recall hushed midnights and rustling oak leaves,
The music so soft only bricks could hear.

The children that live inside old people remember
When the turret of a mighty castle stood in the park.
Musicians launched arrows of song to the sky.
Marches and Viennese waltzes
Fell back to the quilted ground.
Now, on the warm evening breeze
Pigeons coo and fly to the feet of
Old children sitting on park benches.

Her hands are thin as winter branches.
A willow cane roots her to the earth.
A girl's eyes smile through a peeling birch bark mask.
Inside her plays the memory of a white dress she wore
And a rib cage full of drums and tubas and cymbals,
An ocarina and a glockenspiel.
Speaking to pigeons and tossing breadcrumbs,
One old woman taps her foot.

Two-bit Ella

watched her walk to the store;
she wore boots,
carried two bags by the handles,
looked like a scale out of balance.
man, she was old,
walked slow, eyes down,
didn't talk to no one but herself;
white hair blowin' all over.

heard talk about her,
called her Two-bit Ella,
said she took in railroad men,
brakemen, firemen, porters.
the debris that blows down the tracks,
the vagabonds who hide in boxcars
snuck up to her door
when clouds hid the moon.

took 'em inside her coop.
looked like an old railroad shed
invaded by chickens, her house did;
and her yard, well,
what wasn't in her yard?
and all of it broken.

walked by her house at night, curious,
yellow lights behind tattered shades,
two or three fuzzy shadows,
could hear the shadows laugh
till all hours,
till the freight train whistle blew.

drove by this poem not long ago,
poem's gone;
replaced by a rambler, kids, wagons, lilacs,
a different kind of magic.
train whistles are few, most of 'em don't stop,
other night songs in their place.
might be that in a hobo camp somewhere
some old guy remembers.

Juliann Rule

Folks Forget

Town folks said the old man was slow,
but he was never late for a parade;
he dressed militarily (World War I) and
solemnly saluted each passing flag;
he smiled when the marching bands blared,
but he covered his ears and closed his eyes
at every twenty-one gun salute.

That old man should have lead the parade,
but, as always, he was the last sad clown;
no one paid him any mind,
wobbling on his wonderful bicycle,
his bony knees spread wide as he pedaled
his two-wheeled sideshow of streamers and
squirrel tails, reflectors and mirrors,
bells and buzzers and ooga horns.

In this one-story highway town
folks see people come and go, and folks can forget
even an eccentric old man over winter;
when he doesn't appear come Spring
folks often don't even notice
until something seems to be missing
at the end of a parade.

The Collector

A wind-blown old crow at a Dairy Queen
keeps one yellow eye on his bicycle,
its basket full of treasure:
aluminum (good as money), agates,
a rusted carnival button, a broken doll,
a half pint o' rye whiskey.

I wonder where the old crow lives;
I imagine his tarpaper nest
decorated with ribbons and strings,
dog hair and buttons and dragonfly wings,
curtains made of dangly, clangy things
to delight his yellow eye in moonlight.

Jake in the Sun

Look, there's Jake;
sitting in the sun, his eyes closed.
Ah, his leathered face feels warm
as the rusted iron wheels
lying in the grass out behind the grain barn;
warm as Anna's hands used to feel on his skin.

A warm breeze escapes from him, a sigh;
he nods in and out of a birdsong day;
he's tired, and he's got a right to be;
he and Anna built this farm, you know,
long ago, when Sweden was still an ache
in two lovesick, homesick immigrants' hearts.

Now, when noonday sun
has replaced the salt in his eyes;
he remembers when this land lay dying of thirst,
cracked as an old person's skin.
Then the rains came hard, making gullies,
much like tears on a leathered face.

Unknown

White Bread

Ain't no black people
In the Minnesota countryside
Where I live;
No Mexicans, Asians,
Haitians, or Indians.
American white people,
Most with German names,
Live in the frame houses
Along the gravel road
Where I live.
It's not very often
You hear anyone sing out loud
Around here; maybe a child,
But they outgrow it, I guess.
Wish we had some color here;
We're whole wheat, home made,
Strong and good,
But silent as snow.

Old in St. Wendel Township

White hair blowin' all over my face
And winter fingers tell me I'm old;
I can't run the farm by myself,
Hard enough keepin' up with the garden.
Yes, it makes sense, perfect farm sense,
For you and Mary and the boys
To move into the farmhouse, and me
To live in that trailer you bought.
Don't get me wrong, son; without you
This farm would go to the devil,
Or worse, the bank.

It's just that, well,
In that yellow brick farmhouse,
At five minutes to twelve every day,
I hear the clunk of muddy boots
Dropping to the back porch floor.
I smell the seasons in the fields
Walk, stocking-footed, into the kitchen
And mix with the aroma of garden stew.
I feel calloused hands on my shoulders,
A stubbled cheek nuzzling my neck.
It's hard to go, that's all, it's just hard.

Romie's Widow

White-haired and widowed she is.
A person might think such a woman
Would be frail, breeze-blown;
But today, she red-faces into the wind,
Walking like a farmer walks
After a day on the John Deere;
She waves like a farmer waves,
Using all of her arm, same as Romie did.

Juliann Rule

Eggs

Eggs 4 Sale,
Says the widow's sign,
Nailed to a box elder tree.
I wonder who visits her coop;
Maybe a fox who reads between the lines
Of her sign and envisions a hen house feed,
Or maybe the bachelor three farms down,
Who makes no dust on his way to town.
His days, cracked as hard-boiled eggs,
His bachelor nights always scrambled;
He stops because he'd like his life
Sunny side up for a change.

Retired Farmer

Used to be, I'd come in from the barn,
when only the faintest hint of red remained
in the evening sky to greet the stars.
I'd sit on the glider swing,
pull off my boots with a grunt,
drop them, *klunk*, *klunk*, to the floor.
I'd sigh, and bathe my feet in the breeze.
At the sound of my boots dropping,
you came out and rubbed my neck
before we sat together, silently listening
to the chorus of night birds and insects.

Now I sit on a patio, alone
at a retirement home in town,
don't much give a damn about the stars;
they mock the candle flames we call our lives.
The evening songs here are intrusions,
the screams of animals in pain.
I wear these little shoes now,
slippers really, they're so thin.
When I drop them to the floor at night,
they feather to the carpet.
How could you ever hear them fall?

Crops that Grow in a Drought

Ain't nothin' in the rain barrel
But dead flies and dust;
Can't grow nothin'
With dead flies and dust
'cept a temper.

Ain't nothin' in the well
But white bones and stones;
Can't grow nothin'
With white bones and stones
'cept worried.

Ain't nothin' in the sky
But dry wind and sand;
Can't grow nothin'
With dry wind and sand
'cept sorry.

Ain't nothin' left inside me
But a dried-up field.
Can't grow nothin'
In a dried-up field
'cept desperate.

Foreclosure Auction

The combine squats, first in line,
then the tractors and discs and seeders,
the harrow, the spreader, and the eight-bottom plow.
On display for the auction,
they seem to stare the same numb stare
as faces at an orphanage fence.
My wife and daughter and I sit in the pickup,
drink coffee from a thermos,
watch through mercifully steamed windows;
the boys are by the corral, heads hanging,
as the calves are prodded up the chute to the truck.

We're all crying;
and I think these inherited dreams,
first sung in European voices,
these visions of wheatfields, of calloused hands
sculpted to work in earth,
are an inherited sickness;
a sickness of yearning, spoken in bone,
for lush pastures and the seven fat cattle,
for armfuls of children,
joyful and wild as black-eyed susans,
a yearning for dreams, lost to us as yesterday's sun.

Juliann Rule

Lawrence Schug

Dairy Farmers

"Even on the day I die," he told me,
"The cows must be milked on time.
You hear me?
Even on the day I die."

Yesterday's sunrise brought golden light
Through the spider-webbed barn window.
The light embraced him,
Hay dust sparkled like gold dust
Around his bent shoulders.

He sat on this stool yesterday,
Its seat worn smooth long before him
By his father's wool pants.
This stool where I sit,
My head pressed against a Holstein hide.

I remember daddy saying that,
When, a child,
I sat on his lap while he milked.
Like a kitten,
I licked fresh milk from his fingers, son.

In Johnson's Pasture

What it comes down to is a fight
for the apple trees Grandpa Johnson planted;
a fight for cider and blossoms and bumble bees,
for apples that taste like kisses.
That's why, with Orion stalking overhead,
I'm out here in Johnson's pasture
with a gang of farmers and a welder's torch.
That's why some of the men have shotguns,
stand alert for headlights bouncing in the woods.
That's why we're holding up these pieces of roofing tin,
so no one can see the torch
cut through one ankle,
then two, then three steel ankles.
That's why in the morning the powerline people
will find another giant
face down in Johnson's pasture,
one giant step away
from crushing Grandpa Johnson's apple trees.

Abandoned Farm

Two years of drought grayed the house's skin,
But jobs in town broke the windows,
Health insurance and weekends off
Caved in the porch, crushed the glider swing
Where the blue-eyed goldfinch sisters used to sing.

The hayloft is empty of bales and cave boys
Spelunking in tunnels of sweet green alfalfa.
The tractor shed that rumbled
When green and red giants awoke for work
Is sagging from shadowed silence.

A new rotation of crops reclaims the soil,
Summers of sumac, thistle, goldenrod and jewelweed
Replace man-made squares of corn and beans and rye;
The land dresses in a permanence of greens and browns
That have out-lasted the plowman and the plow.

The neighbors hate to even drive by, at first;
But it's been a year, the bank'll never sell the place.
So on an apple crisp September afternoon
The grandma from down the road and her daughter
from town
Pick the Haralsons and Firesides clean as bones.

Juliann Rule

Makin' Hay

Sun set flush
as a farm boy's face;
both been makin' hay
all day.

school bell

was not willow hands
rang this bell.
was strong hands,
a milking girl's hands
rang a call
to young birds and lambs,
spotted colts and black-eyed susans.
was oaken hands
carried in water and built a fire,
caught the sod house children,
taught them to sing like bells
in morning blue prairie air.

The Animals at Margaret's Farm

The ant boys crawl over rusty machinery,
doing a year's field work in an hour;
the farmer ants plow and disc and plant,
harvest a bumper crop of imagination.
In the hayloft there are tunnels and caves
for field mice to explore,
thick, hairy ropes, like spider legs,
hang in sparkling hay dust,
vines no young squirrel could resist.
The young crows tell jokes and cuss,
fight like cats, get dirty as March dogs;
they laugh like chipmunks and
hold their bellies like bear cubs full of summer honey.

Margaret knows how to quiet the young colts;
she reads Black Beauty to them on the glider swing,
or plays her shiny black piano for the little wrens
perched on the piano bench beside her.
Margaret feeds the hungry lambs shade and lemonade,
then leads them through the afternoon breeze
to a soft pasture and quilted dreams
beneath a lullaby willow tree.

Wind in a Remington

Wind
Paints its face
Dakota brown
With topsoil,
Dances the dance
Of prairie fire,
Whistles and snarls
And sweeps confusion
From the plains.

The Roots Know

bare
bleached
bones;
bear,
bison,
beaver,
betrayed
bowmen,
buried
beneath
broken
bluestem,
become
wedded in the wheat.
The
r
o
o
t
s

k
n
o
w

e
r t
o
e
h g
o
w

Bread Bowl

Made of Earth, of clay
Compressed for millions of years
By ocean and mountain and ocean again;
Returned to air and sunlight and water.
Shaped, fired, painted, glazed,
The color of moonlight on rippling water.

The bowl is large; it needs to be,
For it contains all the eye-stretching, golden wheatfields
From Kansas to Saskatchewan,
The blue sky above them,
And sun.

The bowl is generous,
A resting place for running waters,
A chalice filled with the nectar of plum and apple blossoms,
Alfalfa flowers, purple and white;
All the elixirs of forest, hillside, prairie, and garden
That the honeybee's magic can conjure.

The bowl accepts my hands,
Uses my hands to work its magic,
Strong hands,
Knowing, tender, caressing hands,
Made of Earth, of clay.

A Field of Black-eyed Susans

Black-eyed Susan knew she would die
When Prairie Fire returned.
Or perhaps, she would be born.
Birth and death, which is which
Here on the bluestem sea?

Like the snarling, bared-teeth mating of wildcats,
The son of a lusty Dakota wind
Took her with tongue and fingers.
If this is birth, let me live.
If this is death, let me die.

Juliann Rule

The Oglala Aquifer

The limestone shores of the Oglala Sea
Are littered with bones
Older than the red man's bones.
Prairie Fire and Black-eyed Susan
Dance a circle dance on bluestem froth,
Waving tall as men on horseback,
From Oklahoma to Dakota.

Above the Oglala
Blue Sky choreographs Hawk's weave,
But engined men with tunnel eyes
Bring rain without dancing a step.
They've tapped the forgotten limestone past
For the water of ancient storms and glaciers
To fall on perfect circles of wheat.

Black-eyed Susan has moved to a garden in town,
Prairie Fire's dance has been tamed,
The bluestem men were thinned and fenced;
Well points stab deeper in search of the gift
Of the shrunken Oglala Sea.
There is poison in the circle and
Only dust devils dance on salted earth.

Geese

When the wild Canadas return,
bee-hived blue ice
clings to cattail stalks
along the creek.
Drumming wings,
saxophone necks and
bagpipe bodies;
their music,
a Spring concerto,
settles into icy water.

This brassy chorus,
sun-inspired and
clear as blue air,
swells like song from
summer-opened church doors.
The choir glides
across still waters,
singing harmonies
elusive as
Moses crying in the reeds.

Dangerous Crossing

whitetails; single file,
walking with the gait of gandy dancers
on some long-abandoned rail bed,
lay tracks through the tamaracks.
boreal breath trails behind, almost frozen,
drifting into starlight, silver and blue.

the rhythm of hooves and heartbeats,
echoing from nested birches
and naked larches,
cannot distract the horned owl,
yellow eyes focused on the shadow of the mouse.
a neutral moon illuminates a dangerous crossing.

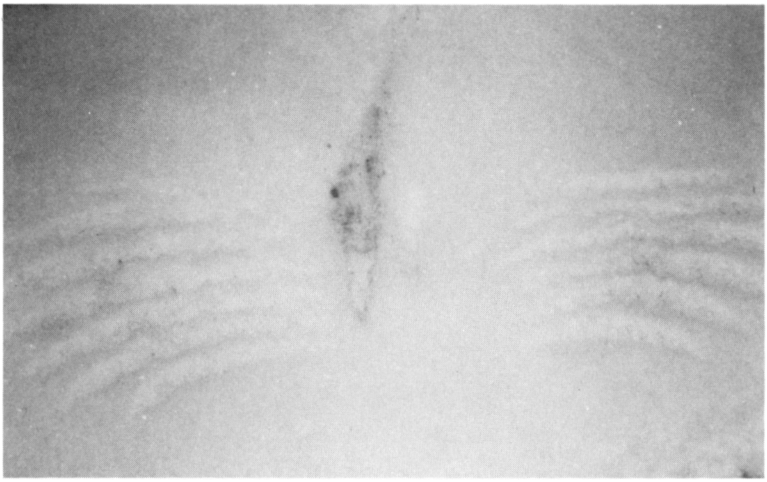

Lawrence Schug

My Ruby Lies Quilted

Shadow blue arcs,
Wind drawn by fine-tipped pens
Of wintergold swampgrass
On diamond-chip snow
Sweep my eyes
To imprint of wing and talon.
A trail of tiny, clawed footprints
Ends in a single ruby of blood.
Naturally,
I am sensitive
To shadows cooling my neck;
I blue sky my eyes too often.
My footprints follow,
Growing larger in the past.
Somewhere, my own ruby lies quilted
In the trackless drifts before me.

Rose-breasted Grosbeaks

We northerners rejoice
As if these migrants are tourists
With money to spend,
And truth be known,
They do make us rich
In the way of a minstrel's tune.
We delight in their song,
So foreign to our winter ears.

But these are no tourists,
These visitors from the south;
They are blood-breasted refugees
Flying from jungle armies,
From loggers of the forest home,
From dammers who silence the river's song.
These birds are survivors of *la revolución*,
Seekers of sanctuary below the northern cross.

For now, they are safe,
They may rest in apple branches.
This summer, their nestlings will fly
Above the lakes and learn the ancient lore
Required for the journey with the sun.
Their migration seems a deportation
To a land whose skin has been burned,
Eroded deeper than buried bones.

A Testimony Against the Witch of St. Wendel

She never spoke it aloud,
Not even to me.
But I saw her one day.
She was crouched down
Where the cotton-tail cats live under water,
Speaking softly in the tongue of the wind.
Smiling,
Nodding,
She spoke the language of orchids.

"The Destruction of the Natural World Is the Destruction of a Personality."

Frances Phillips'
review of *Climbing A Rope Ladder*
by Linda Hogan

Mother Gaia hears each tiny drum
Shudder out of rhythm, then stop.
She gathers fallen wings,
Heavy as earth.
These wings are her burden,
The stones she must carry
In the pockets of her daydream.

Mother collects fish eyes at low tide,
Picks through night's deposit of death
On oil-stinking sand.
She fills a fruit jar with eyes,
Blind, no matter where they look.
These are the eyes
That allow her to see in water dreams.

Mother is a beautiful bag lady
Who collects bleached bones, teeth,
Human tongues and turtle shells;
Squirrel tails and rabbit ears
Bring a smile to her fingers.
Eagle feathers flutter into her grasp;
Gaia gathers the skins of poets and thieves.

No one knows of Mother Gaia's nights,
Where she sleeps, much less the quilt
Made of daydream stones and straw
In which she wraps herself,
Heartsick, grieving as only a planet can.
She offers herself to the sun each dawn,
A lover she knows will kill her in his embrace.

Juliann Rule

A Turtle Poem

The turtle died.
I can tell you that
because this poem isn't about turtles,
though there are turtles swimming around
in this poem;
two snappers, big ones,
so big they must be as old
as the oak trees up on the hill.

One big snapping turtle died,
even though another turtle,
its mate, perhaps,
tried all day, swimming below,
to keep its mossy lover afloat.

What do you think about that?
What was the lesson,
the reason for this poem?

By next morning
the dead turtle had washed up on shore.
Another pretty, pre-historic face
was melting into the peat;
which is reason enough for rhyme.

Eulogy for a Diver

I remember the diver as an aerobat
who leapt from granite ledges
that no other flier would dare.
His arms were extended swan wings;
to the groundlings
the diver hovered in flight
for the length of a summer afternoon
before he speared the water
to the depths of his secret place.

The diver's obituary said he died at home.
I wonder how long he stood alone
on that highest precipice, eyeing the water,
murky for the first time,
before his final dive;
and I wonder if the dive was graceful
or a spasmodic flailing at air,
ending in a splash
forgotten as the water calmed.

I Know Somebody

I know Somebody
who killed Somebody;
five Somebodies,
a covey of quailing farmers.
Somebody killed them with a shotgun
while they ate;
like shooting
a buck and a doe and three fawns
while they grazed at sunset,
hidden in the long shadows
at wood's edge.

Let me tell you all about Somebody,
the killer Somebody.
Twenty years ago or so
Somebody had a Chevy.
Malibu. Blue. Jacked-up. Suped-up.
Chrome wheels. Rubber squeals.
Everybody called him Parnelli.
I don't recall all
the near scrapes and narrow escapes;
Nobody called him Lucky.
Crazy. Parnelli.

Crazy Parnelli Somebody
liked to fight.
When Somebody stepped out of his Chevy
he liked to kick people,
he liked to launch his
wing-tip shoes into face.
But not his friends',
Somebody liked his friends.
His friends like Somebody.
Somebody was a nice guy.

After high school,
Somebody joined the Air Force
while Everybody else
was dodging drafts and faking physicals
or going to college.
Nobody knew why.

Somebody was stationed, probationed
on the high plains of North Dakota,
but he didn't like it.
So Somebody got sick;
he decided to get sick.
Nobody knows how Somebody did it.

Somebody stopped eating, said
he couldn't keep anything down.
And he didn't.
What went down
came up.
The Air Force
called Somebody
Crazy. Sick.

Somebody came home
and decided that, perhaps
he was Buffalo Bill;
long hair, beard, cowboy boots;
fringed and singed.

Somebody lived on a farm
with his friends
and his pinto pony
and his dog
and his friends' dogs.
One night Somebody rode the pinto
into Some town

and pointed a shotgun in the air
and pulled the trigger twice.
Somebody let loose a whoop
and rode out of town on the pinto pony,
right through a cornfield and
Nobody caught Somebody.
Somebody vamoosed.

I was walking through the woods and meadow
at Cowpie Acres with Somebody.
We walked past all these different weeds
and Somebody said you could get high
if you smoke 'em.
The Indians did, he said.

Two days after we sat
with our legs hanging out the hayloft door,
talking about how far down the road
we could see,
Somebody shot his dog.
Then Somebody went hunting
for pheasants
with his father.
On the western prairie of Minnesota,
out where trees live close to farms
but the woods is gone,
Somebody and his father
drove to a farm that
Somebody's father had once owned.
Somebody had lived there as a child.
The farmer said "sure"
Somebody and his father could hunt there.
After the hunt,
Somebody's father went back to the car
with the birds.
Somebody went back to the farmhouse
and made his kill.

Somebody got his limit,
he bagged all five.

Somebody's father heard the shots,
but Somebody said
he was just shootin' up his shells.
So they drove back home,
a regular father and son
on the gravel road,
then the highway.

The next day,
the cops found Somebody
and his bloody clothes and
his red-handed fingerprints.
The judge called Somebody
Crazy. Guilty.
And sent them both to prison.

I saw Somebody only once
after his trial.
I visited Somebody once,
at the state hospital,
at a Valentine's Day party
for the criminally insane.

Everybody was right
about Somebody
a long time ago.
Crazy.

Some seventeen years or so
after the first verse,
some parole board,
some people in some paneled room,
decided Somebody should be free.

Somebody was cut loose, untied.
Somebody split the slammer;
Somebody breathed and blinked
in the bright light.

The other day
Somebody was found
naked and strangled
and tied to his bed.

Some news!
It caused air to catch in some throats,
some eyes to widen,
some heads to shake.

Some talked about justice,
about getting what you deserve,
about living by the sword.
Some may have cried in secret
for Somebody they knew
some time ago.

The Candlemaker's Suicide

In the end
The candlemaker,
A choreographer of flame,
Chose a dark room
For his dance with death.

Blues Shoes

Blues shoes slappin' a highway
carry your beat outa town,
the highway hums
like saxophone wind;
a harmonica train
plays a rumblin' boxcar riff
that gets you to shufflin'.
You grin. Truth is
the blues ain't nothin'
but rocks in your pocket.
You can throw 'em
on the road behind you.

Atlanta, Two a.m., 1967
(My First Plate of Grits)

I've got small-town Minnesota ears,
White ears, hearin' black talk and Lady Soul,
The Temptin' Temptations and James Brown.
The Allman Brothers are cookin'.
Black Faces, black hands; blue smoke
Hangs in this heavy atmosphere.
I've got my white ass glued to a stool,
Quiet, half-afraid, eating my first plate of grits.
I'm breathing as deeply as I can,
Breathing with my eyes and ears and tongue,
Breathing like a poet breathes
When writing poetry without paper.

Anvil

been beat on, man,
wailed on;
my edges
may be round,
but I ain't the one
bein' bent out of shape.

my advice to jim

my advice is
live in a sweat, man,
intense;
moonlit skin
is lovely to smell.
I say
be open-eyed,
open-handed,
open-minded;
microscope your telescope,
tune up your stethoscope.
Be ready
to run in rain,
willow in wind;
jivc in the jungle,
jim.

A Burst of Blue Neon

Clues, hints of you remain fresh on the wind;
your voice speaks heart words
when you fail to guard it closely;
no matter which words you choose to hide behind,
you leave a trail.

Your eyes, when not darting as birds
in a willow thicket, fearful of shadows,
are frozen lakes, mirrors of a glaciered soul
ground down and buried in ice,
dark and groaning for sun.

Your hands, pacing caged lions,
light fires, move from cigarettes to liquor;
they pick up, then discard objects, as if
whatever you lost might be found in your hands,
though what you seek cannot be held.

I can see your gossamer shadow flicker,
a faint light, or perhaps only a hope of light
obscured by silent, lingering ground fog,
yet burning like a burst of blue neon
above the door of your hide-out.

Jumprope

Girl can jump like a robin hoppin'.
When she's feelin' good, you know,
When her knees and ankles are loose,
Her fingers set to snappin',
Her tennies set to tappin' a rhythm
For the twirlers to rap on the street.

When she's jumpin' real good
She sings and claps her hands;
Neighbor ladies come out of their houses
Wiping wet hands on goodwill dresses,
They all sway and clap along, but mama,
She just peeks through the curtains.

When daddy's been drinkin'
That jumprope whistles, sings the blues,
And sometimes mama can't jump fast enough.
Her dance is all backward, she stumbles,
Can't keep no rhythm at all.
The dance floor goes dark and silent.

The neighbor ladies, they hear mama cryin',
Shake their heads at the sound of the blues.
Those women, they turn up their tvs,
Yell at their children to let daddy be.
Night time, they come and wipe mama's tears,
'Cause mama, she always takes care of theirs.

Eleven Days after the Abduction of Jacob Wetterling

I've cried every day for eleven days
Because eleven-year-old boys are poetry,
The metaphor of life itself,
Written in racing bone and blood.
A granite-eyed illiterate,
Unable to comprehend the logic of metaphor,
Is stealing poems at gunpoint,
Tearing pages from their warm chapters.
I've cried every day for eleven days
For every stolen poem, and every poet
Whose book no longer makes sense.

A Prayer

My prayer tonight
Is for the ebon-eyed children
Who wait for prison locks
To rust and fall.
May their cadaverous fathers
Fly as sun blind angels
To the dark cherubim,
Enfold them with ragged wings.
Amen.

Lawrence Schug

Lawrence Schug was born in Glencoe, Minnesota in 1947 and grew up in St. Cloud, Minnesota. He is a graduate of St. Cloud State University and lives, with his wife, in a small house on 55 acres of tamarack bog in St. Wendel Township, Minnesota.